Garden Friends

Ed Ikin

Garden Friends

Plants, animals and wildlife that are good for your garden

National Trust

First published in the United Kingdom in 2012 by
National Trust Books
10 Southcombe Street
London W14 0RA

An imprint of Anova Books Company Ltd

ISBN 9781907892226

A CIP catalogue for this book is available from the
British Library.

20 19 18 17 16 15 14 13 12
10 9 8 7 6 5 4 3 2 1

Reproduction by Mission Productions Ltd, Hong Kong
Printed by 1010 Printing International Ltd, China

This book can be ordered direct from the publisher at
the website www.anovabooks.com, or try your local
bookshop. Also available at National Trust shops,
including www.nationaltrustbooks.co.uk.

CONTENTS

INTRODUCTION

Do we garden alone? It may feel like it as we pore over seed catalogues in the depths of winter, receive no assistance when doing the digging or find ourselves immersed in weeding on a balmy summer's evening. But are we?

The truth is, that no matter how perfectly maintained and contrived our gardens are, we're never alone. Whether we like it or not, we cannot keep nature out of our gardens; after all, we are but one species out of many on this planet. Below our feet, on the plants around us and in the air are a multitude of different organisms and we can chose to embrace or (try to) shun them from our gardens.

Luckily, the choice to garden in harmony with nature is an easy win-win. The enjoyable realisation is that we can have our cake and eat it; we can welcome wildlife into our garden while keeping it looking beautiful, and reap a wide range of benefits bestowed by our guests. How do you improve on the gleaming golden caps of achillea on a warm summer's day? Add some vibrantly coloured hoverflies, buzzing over the flowers, fresh from laying eggs that will soon become aphid-munching larvae. A pond may well be the finishing touch to your garden design, adding a contemplative space, reflecting the colours around it – and, unbeknown to you, attracting slug-eating toads.

This book is about garden friends, a wonderfully diverse array of plants, microorganisms, birds, mammals and invertebrates that help us to maintain a healthy, happy garden while entertaining and inspiring us. It is not about merely letting our gardens go wild for the sake of nature alone. We can still have structure, form, colour, season-round interest, a spot for the deck chair and somewhere to kick a ball around – but with space for shrews, a hedgehog house and a base for bats. The concept of a garden friend is a broad one, and for many, a cold beer and hot bath are their best friends after an exhausting day's digging. However, over the following pages, we'll focus on friends of a natural origin.

PLANTS AND FUNGI

The first chapter looks at some of the alliances that are made between these two kingdoms; symbiotic relationships being fundamental to much plant life on this planet. This chapter also explores companion planting: at its simplest one plant that helps another grow better, although in some cases (such as garlic) this interrelationship can become very sophisticated.

BIRDS AND MAMMALS

Birds and mammals normally occupy the top of any wild food chain, so to see them in your garden is an instant indication of your approach to wildlife. Hedgehogs, song thrushes and shrews all regulate pest levels in different ways and on different scales, and this chapter explores how to encourage them and their useful relatives.

INSECTS AND OTHER INVERTEBRATES

The chapter on insects and other invertebrates focuses mainly on the concept of biological control; using a garden pest's natural enemy to reduce its numbers rather than an insecticide. Not only an elegant solution, but also a highly effective one. This approach always goes beyond merely adding the 'friends' – you have to create the right environment for them to thrive, so you'll find plenty of information about the preferences of lacewings and ladybirds.

AMPHIBIANS AND REPTILES

Amphibians and reptiles add an exotic presence to any garden and their precise habitat requirements mean they won't arrive overnight. However, some simple additions and adjustments to your current environment could bring the rich benefits of a resident toad or slow worm who will both help to keep the numbers of slugs down.

NATURAL INFLUENCES

Finally, the chapter on natural influences looks at yet more steps you can take to improve your garden using the free and effective power of nature.

This is ultimately a practical guide to gardening more harmoniously with nature, but not an exhaustive one. If you feel inspired to attract some new friends into your garden, there can be no simpler principle than understanding your garden's habitat and cross-referencing it with their needs. Some alterations may be simple and effective, others may require lots of work and take many years to be successful but ultimately, even the smallest concession to nature will be deeply rewarding.

The sections at the end of this book will point you towards some of the excellent books, organisations and suppliers who can provide more advice and equipment to help you make expert use of garden friends.

PLANTS AND FUNGI

*How can you make the plants in your garden
work for you? Beyond the visual appeal of flowers
or the crops you grow to eat, there are some amazing
unseen processes going on. Take a look at these
different ways that plants and microorganisms
can help gardeners.*

COMPANION PLANTS

Companion planting is a catch-all term for the different
benefits conferred by bringing combinations of plants
together. In this double act there's invariably a plant of
intrinsic value and a sidekick whose presence enhances the
growth and general performance of the star performer. Often
the companion has a sacrificial role, merely to get plagued by
pests so your main plant doesn't – growing something more
attractive to pests than your crops is about as straightforward
as companion planting comes. Sometimes the relationship is
more sophisticated. Some marigolds, for example, exude a
weed-killing chemical from their roots to suppress even the
most pernicious perennial weeds.

MARIGOLD (*Tagetes* spp.)

Attractive to pest-munching insects, a deterrent to aphids
and the prettiest weedkiller you'll ever use in your garden,
marigolds are bright, breezy additions to any garden.
Operating in a colour spectrum from sunny yellow to brick
red, they grow to 20cm (8in) and look best planted in large

groups. Flowers are borne reliably throughout the summer, generally running out of steam in mid-September.

The easily accessible nectar of the marigold's flowers makes them attractive to many insects, some of which are renowned predators of garden pests. In particular, hoverflies and ladybirds will be attracted to gardens growing marigolds: provide them with nectar and they'll start to investigate other food sources in the garden. Both ladybirds (adults and larvae) and hoverfly larvae are effective 'generalist' predators, able to graze on populations of aphids to stop them reaching critical proportions. The strong odour of the marigold also deters aphids from visiting your crops in the first place.

One particular species, *Tagetes minuta* (see colour section), has a surprising virtue. Its roots excrete a substance that suppresses growth in nearby plants, making it a viable alternative to weedkiller. *Tagetes minuta* is especially effective when planted among perennial weeds: it can weaken or even kill problem plants such as ground elder (*Aegopodium podagraria*), celandine (*Ranunculus ficaria*) and couch grass (*Agropyron repens*) outright. However, the persistence of *Tagetes minuta* itself requires vigilance to stop it becoming a problem; dead-heading the flowers and hoeing off seedlings will ensure it never takes over your garden.

HOW TO GROW: Marigolds can be grown in blocks as part of a display, or around a fruit or vegetable crop that needs particular protection from pests. They tolerate a range of garden habitats, but definitely thrive in full sun. They can grow well on poor soils, and may actually tend to be a little too lush in very rich ground, which may lead to fewer flowers.

Marigolds are tough, reliable plants that are hardy in many climates. For this reason, they can either be direct sown into the soil or raised under glass and planted out in late spring.

If you have the facilities, raising plants in protected conditions (anything from a windowsill to a glasshouse), will even out any climatic variations that may rage outside – it can be frustrating to see heavy rain pounding recently sown soil. Raise seedlings in individual plugs or cells to ensure each plant develops a good root system. Potting up at least once ensures you will have strong specimens to plant out. Hardening off is a vital process to prepare plants raised indoors for a life outside. Once a plant has produced 2–3 sets of 'true' leaves you can gradually reduce its night-time temperature, by moving it to a porch or cold frame. After five days or so of cooler temperatures, and providing no frost is forecast, the plant will be ready for planting.

When sowing direct in the garden, ensure the ground is consistently cultivated, with no big lumps that might force a seedling to grow poorly. Rake the soil level and then mark shallow grooves or drills to sow seed into. Water the bottom of the drill before sowing and drop the seed at regular intervals once the water has drained a little. Rake a thin layer of soil over the seeds to allow them to germinate in the dark. If your seedlings germinate rather thickly, thin them once the 'true' leaves have formed.

Marigolds are rather prone to slugs, so be prepared to launch midnight mollusc-picking patrols, or employ an organic-approved ferrous-sulphate-based slug pellet.

ONION FAMILY (*Allium* spp.)

To the army of invertebrates that populate our gardens, smell is a crucial sense, and may inform their decisions about what to eat as much as sight. This is particularly true for the carrot root fly. This profound irritation to vegetable gardeners has a habit of turning up in the second or third year of a new 'grow your own' initiative. Just as you think vegetable growing is a straightforward business, that most staple of crops, your carrots, appear riddled with a network of black slimy tunnels, often leading into the centre of the root. Once you've removed all the spoilt material, a promising bunch is reduced to a few good carrots.

That distinctive, sweet, starchy carrot aroma guides the carrot root fly towards your crop. Confuse them with one of the simplest, most traditional companion plantings: adding a member of the onion family to your rows of carrots. The pungent scent of chives, onions, garlic or even ornamental plants (such as the dramatic *Allium schubertii*) will do the trick. (Another classic scent-based combination is sage and cabbages, with two strongly alternating aromas deterring classic pests such as caterpillars and leaf-hoppers.)

HOW TO GROW: Simply interplant the two crops, either as alternating rows, or with the stronger-smelling members of the onion family in a defensive ring around the edge of the bed. Chives are best raised from seed and can be sown directly into the soil. *Allium schubertii* and other ornamental onions are best planted as bulbs in the autumn.

Nasturtiums (*Tropaeolum majus*)

Bright, likeable and a clever distraction for troublesome aphids, nasturtiums are annual, scrambling plants, distinguished by bright red or orange trumpet-shaped flowers (see colour section). These colourful plants cover ground rapidly and need very little attention. They're attractive in their own right and the flowers make a delicious, distinctive addition to salads, although they're rather prone to attack from a range of common garden pests. However, it is this quality that makes them the perfect 'sacrificial' plant to grow near prize crops. No matter how attractive your cabbages may have been to blackfly, greenfly and caterpillars, it's a safe bet that they'll prefer nasturtiums. So planting them in a companion capacity is an excellent method for reducing insecticide use while bringing an ornamental, informal quality to your veg patch.

HOW TO GROW: Nasturtiums are fairly tolerant of a variety of garden conditions. While they thrive in hot, sunny spots, they grow reasonably well in semi-shade and can establish in both poor and rich soils. When introducing them to your garden for the first time, it's worth raising good-quality plants from seed in protected (glasshouse or windowsill) conditions if possible. The common nasturtium *Tropaeolum majus* is attractive enough, but it's worth considering cultivars such as 'Alaska Mixed' with a distinctive white marbling on the leaf. 'Whirlybird Cherry' has a silly name but is a lovely shade of rich red, and if you'd prefer a more compact plant and therefore neater look to your companion planting, seek out the dwarf 'Tom Thumb Mixed'. Nasturtiums self-seed readily in the right conditions.

PLANTS TO ATTRACT
FRIENDLY INSECTS

Using plants to lure insects is explored over the next few pages, with a variety of options for every garden and season. Pollinating insects are vital if you are growing crops – no bees means no strawberries. Predatory insects prey on some of the most irritating garden pests – introduce them into your garden and you won't need to rely on pesticide sprays to deal with infestations of aphids.

POACHED EGG PLANT (*Limnanthes douglasii*)

An attractive annual plant that's easy to grow, the poached egg plant attracts several beneficial insects to the garden, to feed from the plant's readily accessible nectaries. It's a breezy, cheery annual from California with striking flowers – five petals splashed with bold blocks of white and gold (see colour section). Its compact shape and abundance of flowers make it perfect for sowing in big, meadow-like drifts at the edge of vegetable beds and borders.

As a perfect nectar source for adult hoverflies, the poached egg plant will attract a potent army of flying predators to help control pests in your garden. Hoverfly larvae make particularly effective aphid predators and once established, will regulate numbers of this pest.

HOW TO GROW: Their home territory, California, provides a good guide. Relatively poor, free-draining soil, full sun and a lack of competition as the plants are establishing are all that is needed. Their willing nature makes you a greener gardener, as once germinated it's unlikely you'll need to resort to any kind of plant care, not even a watering can. Although plants can be started in a glasshouse, they thrive from being sown directly in the soil if conditions are right. Fork over the area to be seeded, ensuring that the soil is open to the full depth of the fork. Rake the soil down to a fairly fine tilth and mark a series of shallow drills. Water the bottom of the drills and when they have drained (and the soil is still damp), sow the seed at 3cm (1¼in) intervals. Cover the drills with soil and thin the seedlings a little when they emerge.

If the soil conditions remain favourable, the poached egg plant should self-seed on a regular basis. Once you can recognise the seedlings, it's simple to restrict them to the desired area. To ensure new plants each year, collect some seed and store in a paper bag in a cool, dry place.

LAVENDER (*Lavandula* spp.)

A plant richly redolent of the Mediterranean with blue to purple flower heads borne on glaucous, aromatic foliage in early to mid-summer. Lavender is one of the great nectar-bearing plants and will attract a vast audience of bees, butterflies and wasps when it flowers. The plant's Mediterranean origins allow it to thrive in exposed situations and it's the perfect plant for poor soil and full sun.

Pore over the bewildering variety of cultivars and species available and chose one to suit your tastes and garden habitat. 'English' lavender (*Lavandula angustifolia*) is generally the most reliable (see colour section), although it loses its appeal as it gets older, becoming 'leggy' with an exposed wooden stem. French lavenders (*Lavandula stoechas*) are now available in some stunning cultivars such as 'Kew Red', 'Regal Splendour' and 'Tiara', but tend to be less hardy. Even more tender is the delicate, beautiful fernleaf lavender (*Lavandula dentata*), perfect for a sunny, frost-free bed.

HOW TO GROW: Lavender should be planted with the minimum of fuss; don't worry about digging organic matter into the soil and additional fertiliser isn't necessary either. If your soil is heavy and prone to waterlogging in the winter but you simply must have lavenders, it's vital to improve the drainage. This can be done by forking in coarse shingle or grit, ideally to two spade's depth. The approximate consistency of the mix should be around one part soil to one part aggregate. A spot in full sun will always encourage the best flowering and growth, although lavender will reluctantly tolerate partial shade.

The best approach with any lavender is to propagate and replace every six to eight years, before the plant becomes too tired. Luckily they're easy to reproduce through cuttings. These should be taken towards the end of the summer, from new season's growth that has just started to stiffen. Using a sharp knife, cut lengths (preferably without flowers on, so they will have more vitality), with the incision just below the bud. Pot in free-draining compost and only mist the cuttings, don't water the compost. If kept in a sunny, frost-free place, cuttings should be rooted by spring.

Butterfly bush (*Buddleja davidii*)

This common, nay ubiquitous, shrub has pale, flaky bark, hairy, glaucous foliage and a cylindrical flower head in a broad range of colours, from pale lilac and deep blue through to white and pink (see below and colour section).

There are few large shrubs that are as easy to grow and so attractive to pollinators, particularly butterflies such as peacocks, red admirals and tortoiseshells. On warm days in mid to late summer, clouds of pollinating insects swarm over the butterfly bush's nectar-rich flowers, making your garden an instant wildlife haven. It's true that the plant's vigour and readiness to self seed can be a little overbearing, but luckily it responds wonderfully to pruning and unwanted seedlings are easy to spot.

HOW TO GROW: The sight of butterfly bushes sprouting over railway sidings indicate that they're not too fussy about where they grow, although the nature of gardening dictates that they won't always establish where you want them to. As a general rule of thumb, free-draining soil and a spot that gets some sun will do the trick.

The main thing is to select the right variety. Pink and lilac are the most attractive colours to pollinating insects, and if you're worried about space, there's a new patio (i.e. extremely dwarf) variety called 'Buzz' that could be grown in a decent-sized container. Butterfly bushes should be pruned hard every spring to maximise the growth of good flowering wood and to stop the shrub becoming too big, woody and tired. In late February or early March, cut down up to a third of the original plant and remove any dead, diseased or damaged wood. If your garden is exposed, bushes can be cut down by half in the autumn to avoid the wind rocking the plant and undermining the roots. Flowers are produced on new season's growth.

HEBE (*Hebe* spp.)

A large and varied genus of tough evergreen shrubs from New Zealand, hebes are particularly happy on windy, exposed sites (actively relishing coastal locations) and take little looking after. Some species are a little coarse, but the charming *Hebe pinguifolia* with rounded, glaucous leaves and the intriguing, wiry *Hebe cupressoides* are both garden plants of high ornamental value. *Hebe* 'Autumn Glory' also highlights another asset of this genus: nectar-rich flowers borne late into the summer and beyond, making them invaluable as a late-season food source for bees.

HOW TO GROW: Hebes grow in a wide range of soils but they don't like excessive waterlogging. They prefer full sun, but can tolerate a little shade. Very hard, persistent frosts may burn the foliage, and hebes tend to get rather 'leggy' after seven to eight years, displaying a rather unattractive bare woody stem under their foliage. Rather than cutting hard back, which tends to kill the plant, take cuttings or replace.

STONECROP (*Sedum* spp.)

These drought-tolerant, semi-succulent herbaceous plants are grown for their late summer flowers and attractive seed heads that can elevate the appearance of a dead winter border. Some of the simpler cultivars such as the classic *Sedum telephium* 'Herbstfreude' (dusty pink flowers that change to red) and 'Purple Emperor' (pinky-red flowers contrasting with rich bronze foliage) are a magnet for insects, particularly the eminently desirable hoverfly.

HOW TO GROW: Sedums will grow in poor ground and like full sun. They tend to be fairly compact and are well suited to the front of a border.

YARROW (*Achillea* spp.)

It's the simple, open, accessible flower structure of yarrow or
Achillea that's so attractive to bees and hoverflies, and the broad
flower heads of this likeable plant are covered with insects on
a sunny day. This plant has many other desirable assets: stiff,
wiry growth that rarely needs staking, a tolerance of relatively
dry conditions and a dazzling suite of colours, the result of
this genus becoming *plant de jour* for nurseries and breeders.
Achillea millefolium provides the origins for a really exciting
new selection of colours: reds are expressed vividly in cultivars
like 'Paprika' and 'Red Velvet', yellows in the classic 'Cloth
of Gold' and newer 'McVities' and nicely contrasting burnt
oranges in the lovely 'Terracotta'. Achillea is a herbaceous
perennial best bought from a nursery that stocks a wide
range of the many cultivars available – why limit yourself?

HOW TO GROW: Establish plants in ground improved with
a little organic matter that gets plenty of sun.

LIGULARIA (*Ligularia* spp.)

Ligularia will produce strong green or bronze foliage and
cheery, dramatic flowers. This display does not go unnoticed
by bees, wasps and hoverflies who flock to them in droves.
Two classic, complementary cultivars are *Ligularia dentata*
'Desdemona' (with green leaves) and 'Othello'. Growing to
a dramatic 2m (80in) or more in damp ground, this is a
statement plant, grown for height or to patrol the back
of a herbaceous border.

HOW TO GROW: This plant likes to have wet feet. Grow in boggy ground or near a pond's edge, with plenty of space in full sun (although part-shade is tolerated). Be ready to stake plants if the growth is strong.

LUNGWORT (*Pulmonaria* spp.)

Lungwort is an underrated genus with an unfair reputation for being plain and coarse. With the right varieties, lungwort can bring real panache to the late winter/early spring garden and offers an invaluable source of nectar to early emerging insects. Striking cultivars such as 'Blue Ensign' never get too unruly, and bear a really rich colour in their flowers, almost unmatched in late winter.

HOW TO GROW: Best planted in larger groups of 12 or more plants, lungworts are happiest in part shade and growing in soil enriched with a little leaf mould or compost.

It's worth visiting nurseries who specialise in shade-loving perennials to look at new varieties. Recent breeding has put more emphasis on richer colours and finer foliage.

HEATHER (*Erica* spp.)

Heather is another underrated group of plants, still recovering
from excessive use in the 1970s heather/conifer combo seen
in many suburban gardens. The truth is that heathers are
available with a fantastic range of flower and foliage colours
and habits ranging from prostrate to wild and bushy. More
importantly, on the first warm day of spring, sometime around
early March, your heathers will be alive with bees that have
seemingly appeared from nowhere. *Erica vagans* can tough out
drier conditions that most, while some of the cultivars, such
as *Erica* x *darleyensis* 'Kramer's Red' are genuinely dramatic,
showy plants.

HOW TO GROW: Heathers grow naturally on sandy soil,
and this is undoubtedly where they're happiest. When
young, heathers have little resistance to drought and need
to be watched diligently in dry summers. Planting and
mulching with well-rotted leaf mould greatly assists with
their establishment.

GREEN MANURES

Green manures are the other main category of friendly plant, although this term somewhat sullies an attractive group of plants. Their main role is to screen bare soil from the elements. When soil is left bare, wind and rain can cause compaction or actually wash soil away. All green manures have a simple 'umbrella' effect, the leaves deflecting the worst wind, rain and snow from the ground and helping to minimise erosion and 'leaching' (the loss of vital nutrients from the soil). Simply by growing, they also stop weeds from getting a foothold. There's nearly always a secondary benefit, from attracting bees to making nitrogen useable in the soil to boost the growth of subsequent plantings. Most green manures are simply dug back into the soil in spring.

PHACELIA (*Phacelia tanacetifolia*)

There are three good reasons for growing phacelia in your garden. The speed at which it can germinate and grow prevents unused soil from staying bare and attracting weeds, making it the perfect green manure to span the gap between a winter and summer/autumn crop, such as winter cabbage and autumn carrots. The second benefit is the ameliorating quality of the roots on garden soil; their fine fibres grip the structure, keeping it fine and crumb-like, rather than leaving thicker clods or plates. The final purpose of phacelia is its trump card over other green manures: its attraction for bees. It's one of the main 'fodder' crops for commercial bee production; its ready source of nectar will encourage a balanced ecology in your garden and attract bees to help with pollination.

A member of the borage family with coarse, hairy foliage and deep bluey-purple flowers, phacelia is striking but robust (see colour section). Able to grow quickly, you can forgive its slightly coarse, sprawling habit for its free-flowering nature. It 'goes over' quickly, but can respond to a hard, prompt shearing back.

HOW TO GROW: Phacelia is not fussy, growing on a wide range of soils, although less happy on heavy, boggy ground. Full sun encourages good flowering and, consequently, visiting bees, although it will tolerate some shade at the beginning and end of the day. Sow seed direct into beds and borders from mid-spring onwards; there is little to be gained by starting such a vigorous plant under glass. Sow into shallow drills, in well-cultivated soil and remove competing weed seedlings. By making parallel drills, it's easy to spot your desirable seedlings as they emerge. Phacelia could easily self-seed in the right conditions, although, of course, it may not come up where you'd like it. By collecting seed when it's dry and ripe, you can re-sow in the desired location the following year.

Broad beans (*Vicia faba*)

Easy to grow and willing to germinate in the autumn, these
terrific plants cover and improve soil that would otherwise
remain bare over winter. Occasionally referred to as field
beans, broad beans are one of the stoutest, most reliable
garden crops. There are few plants quite so willing to
germinate and grow through the course of a miserable autumn
or winter, and this alone endears them to the gardener. Strong,
stout stems and rounded, slightly glaucous foliage distinguish
broad beans, and if sown in September or October, they can
be 1–1.2m (3–4ft) tall by late spring.

There are two additional qualities that distinguish the
broad bean. Its roots are particularly effective at unbinding
the soil – maintaining an even, crumbly structure – and this
leaves the ground extremely easy to cultivate afterwards.
Another reason to grow broad beans is a remarkable one:
they can fix nitrogen in the soil. Or, to be more accurate,
they can convert nitrogen into a form that helps plants
grow. Broad-bean roots feature nodes filled with a bacteria
called *Rhizobium*. These microorganisms have the ability to
turn the relatively toxic, insoluble and unstable nitrite form
of nitrogen into the far more nutritious, soluble and useful
nitrate, the equivalent of the nitrogen fertiliser purchased
in a garden centre.

When beans are growing vigorously, nitrate is actively being
generated in the soil, greatly improving fertility and leaving
ideal conditions for your next crop. No crops are precluded
from following beans in traditional crop succession, and
anything that is prized for its leafy growth will benefit in

particular. For this reason, consider following beans with cabbages, broccoli, lettuce or Brussels sprouts.

HOW TO GROW: Broad or field beans grow readily in a wide range of soils. If you actually want to harvest beans from your green manure, exposure to sun encourages pollinators and helps pods to ripen. However, if you plan to dig your green manure back into the soil before this, you can grow bean plants in relatively shady conditions.

For the most effective winter green-manure effect, sow in late September or early October, when the ground is moist and still fairly warm. Soaking the beans overnight in water in a warm, sheltered spot seems to break down the seed coat and leads to speedier germination – vital if winter is closing in. If beans are laid into well-cultivated ground in drills 2–4cm (¾–1½in) deep, they will germinate quickly, establish before the coldest weather and grow rapidly as soon as the warmth of spring comes. Later sowings are possible – broad beans have a remarkable ability to start growing in the midst of a winter thaw. Autumn-sown beans are less prone to blackfly than spring-sown as their growth is wiry and tough when these pests hatch out, thwarting their attempts at sucking bean sap. Pinching out soft growing tips will offer further protection from blackfly and make a bushier plant.

PLANTS AS PESTICIDES

Garlic (*Allium sativum*)

One of nature's most effective pesticides, garlic is a hardy, bulb-forming perennial that has been cultivated globally for food and medicine for millennia. Long, thin leaves are borne from a broad white bulb and followed by spherical flowers (see page 30 and colour section).

Garlic could rightfully claim to be one of the friendliest plants at the disposal of the organically minded gardener. All of the pungent flavour in the bulb, which so polarises people in terms of taste, has some profound origins. Garlic is comprised of a heady biochemical cocktail. One of its key components, allicin, is proven to have antibiotic, antifungal and insecticidal properties, making garlic a key weapon in the chemical-free maintenance of your garden. Harness these properties either through companion planting or application as a liquid preparation. Regular applications of garlic will control blackspot levels on your roses, keep rust and mildew away from lettuces, tomatoes and cabbages and suppress soil-borne diseases such as *Pythium* (the 'damping-off' fungus that kills seedlings) and *Rhizoctonia* (which kills woody plants like heathers). The element selenium is a key constituent of allicin and is also a vital trace element (minor nutrient) for plant growth.

A home-made garlic solution should follow the ratio of one large bulb to ½ litre (1 pint) of water. Crush the bulb to release as much allicin as possible and steep for 12 hours. Dilute one part garlic solution to ten parts water.

Alternatively, buy some ready made. Professional garlic formulations are available either at larger garden centres or by mail order. Generally sold under rather ambiguous brand names, a quick check of the ingredients will reveal the presence of garlic concentrate. Apply regularly to crops and ornamental plants that are prone to disease, following the dilution recommended by the manufacturer and allowing the liquid to drip off the edge of the leaf. The concentrate is extremely strong; never inhale it in an enclosed area, your nostrils will not forgive you; and be prepared for a distinctive aroma to hang over your garden for a few hours after application.

If you use beneficial mycorrhizal products (see page 39) to boost plant growth in your garden, it's worth remembering that for all of garlic's organic wholesomeness, it will kill fungi, either good or bad. For this reason, never apply the two products together, as they'll cancel each other out.

The use of garlic is not just limited to small-scale domestic gardening; the narrowing range of pesticides available and the growing interest in organic food make professional formulations of garlic a key weapon for commercial gardeners and growers.

HOW TO GROW: Garlic is tolerant of many soils and climates, although as a cultivated crop it really thrives in richer soils and warmer late summers. It's best to avoid extremes of temperature to ensure it retains its properties when you make up a liquid preparation.

Garlic can be raised from seed, either in modules in a glasshouse or in well-cultivated soil after the main threat of frost has passed. However, the most success is generally had with sets: individual cloves planted in the ground, which bulk up to form bulbs by the end of the growing season. Sets are often heat-treated, which reduces the risk of bolting (flowering fast without producing a decent bulb), and can be planted either in autumn or spring. Bolting is often a reaction to stress, with the plant deciding to invest energy in seed (to ensure a new generation) rather than an energy-rich bulb. Avoiding drought stress will further reduce bolting.

The popularity of garlic has led to a huge variety of cultivars, from the compact 'Venetian' to the monstrous 'Elephant'.

To use garlic as a companion plant, it needs to grow effectively around the roots of the plant it's protecting. In a systematic process, the compounds produced by the garlic roots are absorbed by the companion and transported around its vascular system, ensuring a garlicky experience for any pest attempting to eat it. For this reason, choose a garlic cultivar that will complement, rather than swamp the plant it's protecting – coarser varieties, particularly wild garlic, can become a weed in the wrong place.

PLANTS THAT DO THE WORK FOR YOU

POTATOES (*Solanum tuberosum*)

The perfect start for a run-down allotment, these vigorous members of the nightshade family are a staple food, providing good levels of carbohydrate and an underrated source of vitamin C. Forming starch-rich tubers around a large, wiry root system, potatoes' extensive foliage starts to die back as its crop becomes ready (see colour section).

Potatoes are often billed as a great 'cleaner' of the soil, although much depends on the toil of the gardener involved! The benefits start with the amount of soil cultivation required to get seed potatoes established, necessitating a thorough removal of perennial weeds from the ground. As the potatoes become established, their wiry, extensive root systems break down heavy clods of soil associated with poorly cultivated ground, leaving behind a terrific medium for growing more delicate crops.

HOW TO GROW: To ensure a decent crop of potatoes, plant in plenty of open ground and deep soil. Full sun encourages strong growth and a good crop.

Start off seed potatoes by setting them out in egg boxes, in a cool but light place (a shed or unheated room) where they will start to develop shoots – a process known as chitting. Meanwhile, clear all perennial weeds from your plot, fork the ground thoroughly and draw the earth into furrows, with plenty of space between each one. Plant your seed potatoes, shoots facing upwards at 30cm (12in) intervals and cover with soil. As the plants grow, earth them up by drawing more soil around the roots: this reduces the chances of your crop going green and becoming inedible. Harvest once the foliage starts to die back, although they stay remarkably fresh if left in the ground into autumn and early winter. Salad crops find the finely crumbed soil left behind by potatoes easy to grow in and root vegetables such as carrots and parsnips will be able to push through the open soil readily.

CROP ROTATION

As your allotment or vegetable plot continues, consider rotating your crops to stop serious diseases becoming resident in the soil. Vegetable crops fall neatly into several families: *Apiaceae* (carrots, celeriac, parsnips), *Brassicaceae* (cabbages, broccoli, rocket), *Fabaceae* (beans, peas and other legumes), *Solanaceae* (potatoes, peppers, tomatoes) and *Asteraceae* (lettuce). By growing each family group in one plot for a limited time – say one or two seasons – there won't be the time for the diseases associated with it to build to critical levels.

YELLOW RATTLE *(Rhinanthus minor)*

If your early attempts at establishing a wild-flower meadow merely look like an overgrown lawn, the problem may be simple: excess fertility in the soil. If the ground is too rich, particularly in nitrogen, only the most vigorous plants (typically perennial grasses, docks and nettles) will reign, excluding more delicate and interesting species.

Soil fertility can be reduced in several ways. Cutting and collecting the cut foliage every year is a key part of your approach (nitrogen is removed with each cut and collect). However, a head start can be gained by sowing yellow rattle into the sward. A member of the *Orobanchaceae* family, yellow rattle is a subtle plant with serrated leaves and bright yellow flowers (see colour section). This unassuming plant is normally a grass parasite (although it can grow without a grass host) and takes nutrients and sugars from a grass plant's root system, greatly reducing its vigour and limiting its dominance over other species. With the vigour of the grasses reduced, a more level playing field is created, which allows delicate meadow species, such as cornflower, spotted orchid, viper's bugloss and ox-eye daisy an opportunity.

HOW TO GROW: Yellow rattle is a native of meadow grassland in open, sunny sites. It may not grow so well in very heavy, waterlogged soil. Seed is widely available from mail-order wild-flower and meadow specialists. The next step is to create opportunities in your grass for it to establish. Do this from early September to late October, when the soil is moist but still warm from the summer. Digging out perennial weeds such as dock and dandelion will leave some enticing bare soil in which to introduce yellow rattle. Scratching or scarifying your meadow, either with a spring-tine rake or a pedestrian scarifier (you can hire one) is the next step, ripping out lumps of grass and extending your potential seed bed. Press the seed lightly into the ground, but don't cover it. It should germinate readily, although the chances of this are improved if the soil is moist and open in structure. If the winter is harsh or the following summer excessively dry, you may need to sow again.

When cutting your meadow, wait until the end of the summer and check that all the wild-flower (including yellow rattle) seedheads have set seed and are dry. Cutting prematurely will stop the full range of meadow plants from seeding and diversity will start to drop.

PLANTS FOR BIRDS

Should we provide extra food for birds to eat in the garden, potentially making them too dependent on us for nutrition and adversely affecting their 'natural' diet? A good compromise is to offer natural sources of food that promote normal feeding behaviour, suited to the ecology of the birds in your garden. Freshly dug ground will offer worms for robins and blackbirds, while native, but garden-worthy plants such as teasels provide a plentiful source of seeds for finches.

Some plants, of course, are multipurpose. Ivy is a great source of nectar for bees and other insects, including moths. Flowering in September and October, the berries ripen in February and are favoured by blackbirds and other birds who also rely on ivy for shelter and nest sites.

TEASEL (*Dipsacus fullonum*)

A vigorous, spiky thistle-like plant native to Britain, the teasel is one of the great 'architectural' plants with a wiry, sculptural quality that endures long after the plant has died (see colour section). Teasels are often at their most striking on a frosty winter morning, preferably with a spider's web or two hanging off for extra dramatic effect. Teasels are biennial plants, so seedlings have a year of purely vegetative growth and the flower stem is produced the following year before the plant dies. The dense seed heads, borne from late summer into early winter, can attract dramatic, chattering flocks of finches, including the beautiful goldfinch. The oil-rich seeds make a calorie-packed meal for birds bracing themselves for winter.

HOW TO GROW: Teasels prefer slightly damper ground, although they don't mind full sun, and they're the ideal thing to grow near a pond or a boggier part of your garden. Getting teasels to become a regular feature shouldn't be too difficult, given their vigour and extremely effective seeding mechanism. Seed is available from both wild-flower specialists and more general nurseries. This should be sown in late spring into well-prepared ground that has preferably been lightly forked over then raked down to even tilth.

There's every chance that this is all you need to do to have teasels in perpetuity. They have the scope to become 'weeds', such is their willingness to self-seed. Sowing the teasel in the right spot is crucial – it's unfair to expect perfect behaviour in a well-mannered herbaceous border. Give it a wild area and let it proliferate. If you want to halt its spread, seedlings are easy to spot and remove.

IVY (*Hedera helix*)

A familiar sight, ivy is a glossy-leaved climber capable of growing in conditions no other plant will tolerate, including deep shade. Its strong, grasping roots allow it to climb smooth walls, leaving a permanent impression on render and brick (see colour section).

For some, ivy has no place in a garden, and it's true it can lend a rather scruffy, derelict air when used indiscriminately. It rarely works well as a ground cover, as it's invariably more vigorous than neighbouring plants. However, in some situations, ivy is a most useful garden friend, and can become a mini ecosystem.

Extremely rich in nectar, easy to access and borne in abundance, ivy flowers are a magnet for pollinators, and being a native species, there's a high degree of compatibility with many insects. Flowering from September and into October, ivy will be a major food source in your garden in the second half of the year, providing nectar long after other plants have died back.

The dull black berries, also available in large quantities, provide one of the few reliable sources of winter nutrition for thrushes and pigeons. Its tough glossy leaves may look unpalatable, but are a primary food source for several species of moth caterpillar including the swallowtailed moth (*Ourapteryx sambucaria*) and small dusty wave (*Idaea seriata*).

The dense, twining nature of ivy makes it a terrific refuge for a large range of wildlife, providing nesting sites for blackbirds, song and mistle thrushes, which occasionally nest on the ground where the cover is dense enough. It is ideal cover for smaller birds seeking a secluded roosting spot. Training ivy around the edge of open-fronted bird boxes provides extra seclusion and reassurance for vulnerable birds like robins, wrens and pied wagtails.

HOW TO GROW: Ivy is one of the toughest, least fussy plants you could grow in your garden. Happy in full shade or sun, rich soil or free-draining sand, it's actually quite an achievement to kill it.

While ivy can become a weed in some situations, it is important to define its place in your garden and allow it to thrive there. This is straightforward, as, although tenacious, ivy should be easy enough to remove from any area where you don't want it, thanks to a fairly shallow root system.

The best way to accommodate ivy in your garden is to allow it to climb or sprawl, either over a structure or up a tree. There is much myth and nonsense espoused about ivy 'killing' trees. This is simply not true. The two disadvantages of ivy growing on trees are: one, it can hide decay and the fruiting bodies of fungi that may be causing the tree harm; and two, in extreme cases, the weight of excessive ivy may place strain on a weak tree's structure. On a healthy tree, ivy is perfectly acceptable, particularly if you have time to rein it in once a year and remove excess growth. Avoid cutting ivy foliage during the summer, to allow the nectar-rich flowers to develop in the late summer, also one of the plant's most attractive features.

Ivy can be used creatively to create habitats for birds: grow it on a 'tunnel' of low hoops (these could be made simply by bending over flexible bamboo canes, although more substantial metal ones could be purchased) to offer a camouflaged retreat for occasional ground nesters such as thrushes and blackbirds – though this is not a good idea if cats and/or rats abound.

MYCORRHIZAL FUNGI AND MICROBES

Appearances can be deceptive. While it may look like our plants grow in isolation, they actually interact with a multitude of microorganisms in the air and soil. Although fungi and bacteria are sometimes thought of simply as diseases, they form close, mutually beneficial associations with a wide range of plants, to the extent that some partners cannot exist without the other.

A hidden ally for many of your plants, mycorrhizal fungi are thin, thread-like fungi that live exclusively in the soil. Then there are disease-suppressing bacteria and a wide range of symbiotic microbes, some of which are unequivocally friendly. Luckily they're easy to introduce to your garden.

Mycorrhizal fungi

Mycorrhizal fungi are soil dwellers, types of mainly friendly symbiotic fungus distinguished by long thin tendrils that weave their way through the earth, looking for suitable associates, or victims, depending on the species. They should not be confused with other pathogenic mycorrhizal fungi, such as honey fungus (*Armillaria* spp.), whose thick, black 'bootlaces' are easy to spot on dead wood, crawling up just inside the bark.

Desirable mycorrhizal fungi bring many benefits to a garden soil. When they associate with plant roots, they can increase the roots' mass and efficiency, making for better uptake of water and nutrients. Their presence in the soil can also deter disease-bringing pathogenic fungi, maintaining a healthy balance impossible to replicate through a chemical-based gardening regime.

HOW TO USE: A healthy, balanced soil with a good volume of organic matter is essential. Mycorrhizal fungi are intrinsic to all 'wild' soils and exist in a wide variety of habitats, but garden soils can be less supportive to mycorrhizal fungi, particularly if they've been managed intensively. Traditional garden operations like digging, using synthetic fertiliser, weedkiller and growing a single crop intensively, year in, year out, can impoverish soil quality and deter mycorrhizal fungi from establishing. In this situation, the soil is open to invasion from other, disease-causing (pathogenic) fungi that will attack the resident plants.

While it may not be possible to create a perfect wild soil in your garden, such simple measures as preventing it from being bare during the winter, adding copious volumes of high-quality organic matter, using organic fertilisers (if you need to use fertilisers at all) and minimising the use of pesticides and weedkillers will encourage mycorrhizal fungi to colonise your soil.

You can also boost the soil content by actually adding mycorrhizal fungi that have been isolated and incorporated into organic granules. These are now widely available in garden centres under various brand names. Granular mycorrhizal fungi can be dug into the ground prior to planting and added as a top dressing around trees and shrubs two or three times during the growing season.

Planting bare-root roses, trees or shrubs gives you the perfect opportunity to coat their roots in mycorrhizal fungi to aid rapid establishment. Buy the fungi in the form of a root-dip – a powder that becomes a thick gel when mixed with water. By dunking the plant's roots directly into a bucket of the gel before planting, you're maximising exposure to the beneficial microbes – this can be more effective than adding a handful of granules to the planting hole.

Whichever sort you buy, follow instructions on the bag carefully. Only buy what you need for that growing season, as the fungal culture can fade away if the product is stored for more than six to eight months.

'FRIENDLY' BACTERIUM (*Bacillus subtilis*)

A soil-dwelling bacterium, only visible through the microscope, *Bacillus subtilis* is a natural ally of plants and is found in abundance in any wild soil. Recent advances in crop science have not only worked out how it can benefit gardeners, but have also isolated it into an easy-to-use consumer product.

Bacillus subtilis is a friend to plants and an enemy to many pathogenic (i.e. disease-bearing) bacteria and fungi. By rapidly occupying the root space around plants, it out-competes aggressive pathogens and actually manufactures its own antibiotic to help either eliminate or suppress them. *Bacillus* also feeds on the starches produced by plants as a by-product of respiration (the plant's way of generating energy), which might otherwise attract pathogenic fungi and bacteria into the root zone of the plant. Proper, timely use of *Bacillus* can eliminate the need for 'conventional' fungicides. Liquids containing *Bacillus* are the first 'biological' product approved for use as a fungicide.

HOW TO USE: *Bacillus subtilis* will establish in any reasonably warm garden soil or compost and is approved for use in both glasshouse and garden. Buy it as a concentrated liquid under various brand names. Diluted down and added as a drench directly to the soil or direct to foliage, it will either inoculate against the threat of disease or act directly on an existing infection such as powdery mildew.

When propagating young plants, add *Bacillus* to seed trays prior to sowing or to a compost mix for cuttings. Apply again when the plants are subjected to stress, such as being pricked out or potted-on. Using *Bacillus* at the first sign of disease – for example, when small blisters or pustules develop on leaves, in the case of rust – can arrest the symptoms and encourage the plant to develop resistance. As a fungicide, *Bacillus* is relatively gentle in its action and may struggle to overcome excessive, late-stage infection, so vigilance and some knowledge of early symptoms is useful.

GARDEN AND GLASSHOUSE HYGIENE

While new products are liberating gardeners from conventional fungicides, there are many basic rules of garden and glasshouse management that foster good hygiene and allow the likes of *Bacillus* to work more effectively and efficiently.

Glasshouses need good ventilation; decent airflow will reduce the humidity that allows fungal spores to reach critical mass. It's worth knowing the minimum temperatures plants will tolerate, to help you decide when to open the vents. Out in the garden, plants need ventilation too; try to plant disease-prone shrubs, such as roses, in exposed spots with good airflow, and never allow the centres of woody plants to become congested. Prune strategically to outward-facing buds to create open structures, where diseases will struggle to fester.

Stagnant water acts as breeding ground for pathogenic bacteria and fungi (not to mention undesirable insects such as mosquitoes), and should never be tolerated in a glasshouse. In this setting, dead plant material should also be eyed with suspicion, given its capacity to support fungal diseases. Take this approach outside too, around your roses; limit the opportunities for diseases to breed and there's every chance you'll need to intervene less.

BIRDS AND MAMMALS

Sensitive to habitat destruction and loss of traditional food sources, mammals and birds often see our gardens as places of refuge where they can survive, eat and breed successfully.

The role of gardens in nature conservation is increasingly recognised by wildlife surveys, indicating the richness and diversity of species that gardeners can support – and contradicting the notion of gardens as ecological 'black holes'. However, it's not just our conscience that's satisfied when we create a good hedgehog habitat – we can draw on their friendly qualities to control pests. Snails meet their nemesis in the form of song thrushes, while shrews happily eat slugs.

With so many birds requiring a habitat reminiscent of a woodland glade, comprising both trees and open grass, is it any wonder that our gardens prove such a desirable habitat? The most common misconception about wildlife gardening is that it needs to be wild. Of course it's important to incorporate native plants, although this can be done creatively, but exotic plants and good design needn't be off the menu entirely. It's the diversity found in the best wildlife gardens that makes them so attractive to birds, with a wide variety of food, and plenty of places to perch and nest.

Hedges are a more bird-friendly barrier than panel fences, allowing freedom of movement for garden birds while sheltering them from airborne and ground predators. Hedges provide excellent nesting sites for vulnerable wrens and

Phacelia (*Phacelia tanacetifolia*)

Yellow rattle (*Rhinanthus minor*)

Butterfly bush (*Buddleja davidii*) with tortoiseshell butterfly

Nasturtium
(*Tropaeolum majus*)

arlic (*Allium sativum*)

Potato (*Solanum tuberosum*)

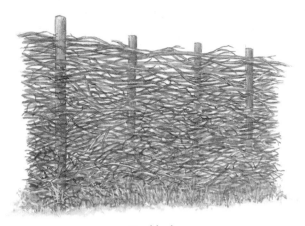

Dead hedge

Ivy (*Hedera helix*)

Teasel (*Dipsacus fullonum*)
with goldfinch

Marigold (*Tagetes minuta*)

Poached egg plant (*Limnanthes douglasii*)

Lavender (*Lavandula angustifolia*)

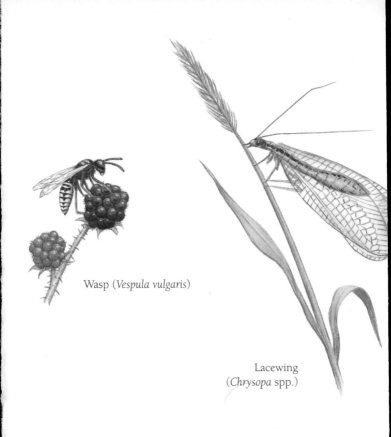

Wasp (*Vespula vulgaris*)

Lacewing
(*Chrysopa* spp.)

Seven-spot ladybird
(*Coccinella septempunctata*)

Song thrush
(*Turdus philomelos*)

Robin (*Erithacus rubecula*)

Chickens (Dorking cockerel and hen)

Hedgehog
(*Erinaceus europaeus*)

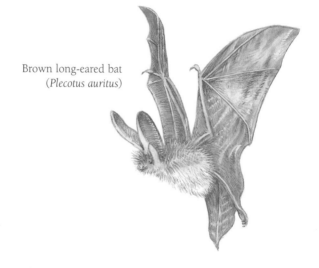

Brown long-eared bat
(*Plecotus auritus*)

Common shrew
(*Sorex araneus*)

Hoverfly (*Episyrphus balteatus*)

Stag beetle (*Lucanus cervus*)

Toad (*Bufo bufo*)

dunnocks, while rooks prefer the most prominent spot possible at the top of your tallest tree.

A simple awareness of feeding differences between common birds will help you plan your garden. Finches use strong beaks to eat seeds, thrushes prefer berries and invertebrates, while martins and swallows catch insects on the wing, often over water.

The presence of raptors such as sparrowhawks in gardens is an emotive one, and there's strong debate about whether they plunder songbird populations, although the law unequivocally protects them. This is ultimately nature in its purest form – and both the skill and drama of the raptor, and the resilience of the songbird should be admired and tolerated. If not, a number of harmless, humane raptor repellents exist to deter them from your garden.

Chickens are a regular sight in many urban and rural gardens. While their eggs and bohemian character are reason enough to keep them, they can also prove to be effective pest-management devices. There's an introduction to keeping them in this chapter (see page 57).

MAMMALS

HEDGEHOG (*Erinaceus europaeus*)

These shuffling, nocturnal mammals' pointed snouts and prickly covered backs make them instantly recognisable, and they're a relatively common member of our British fauna (see colour section). Luckily for the gardener, hedgehogs eat caterpillars and slugs, and can eat half their body-weight – ½kg (1lb)! – in garden undesirables in a single night. In addition to this, their diet is truly omnivorous, and they act as a vital cog in the food chain.

Hedgehogs can really thrive in gardens, and not just 'wild' ones that have sacrificed everything to nature. The key, as with wildlife gardening, is diversity – choosing your design and planting carefully to create a wide variety of habitats and food. As a potentially vulnerable, nocturnal mammal, it's vital that hedgehogs have a safe, reliable shelter for daytime sleeps and, ideally, winter hibernation. As you might expect, they prefer somewhere that's dry, secluded from predators and relatively warm. Plenty of dead wood ensures lots of hideouts, both for sleeping and sheltering if disturbed. Their limited mobility (an inevitable consequence of their endearing short legs) means gardens with sharp changes in level can pose a risk, putting the hedgehog in danger of falling and getting stuck. Gentle transitions and a ramp here and there will create a less threatening topography.

HOW TO ENCOURAGE THEM: The hedgehog's varied diet requires diversity in the garden. Dead wood for beetles, nectar-rich plants for insects and water for refreshment may convince them that your garden is a desirable residence. If you think hedgehogs are present in your garden, you can buy a hog house to provide a tailor-made shelter – although well-built 'dead hedges' or wood stacks (see page 79) are also attractive options. Similarly attractive are the lovely big stacks of wood that get constructed around November 5th, although the hedgehog moving in for the winter won't realise it's shortly to go up in flames. Check your bonfire thoroughly to make sure no one's in residence before the big night.

As hedgehogs prepare for winter hibernation, their thoughts turn to the high-fat diet required to get them through to spring. Wildlife experts agree that this is a good opportunity to provide supplementary food. The old cliché of feeding hedgehogs bread and milk is a myth and can actually cause upset stomachs – the bacteria in milk is potentially lethal in high doses. A much safer bet is cat or dog food, which is rich in fat and offers plenty of calories.

BATS (various spp.)

What was that dark shape flickering past the window?
Bats are more common and more closely linked to human
habitation than many think and are a regular sight at dusk,
both in town and the country. Britain is host to 18 species,
from the diminutive pipistrelle to thrush-sized serotine and
the brown long-eared bat (see opposite and colour section).
Their populations are under great pressure from housing
developments and changes in land use.

Bats have a curious hold on our psyche, and to someone who
has studied and observed them closely, the idea of fearing a
bat is hard to comprehend. They're a highly desirable presence
in your garden. Forming a nocturnal insect patrol, bats are
ruthlessly effective hunters of moths, gnats and mosquitoes,
using sophisticated echo-location and dazzling turns of speed
to silently catch their prey. Bats sit at the top of their food-web
(the complex interrelationship between predators and prey)
and their absence can lead to a proliferation of their quarry.

HOW TO ENCOURAGE THEM: Bats need both day roosts
to rest before their nocturnal hunting begins and large
maternity roosts where females can raise young in safe,
warm conditions. Old barns and large attics offer the perfect
environment for maternity roosts, and some houses may have
80 to 100 bats happily co-existing with the human residents.
Away from domestic dwellings, ancient trees are the traditional
'wild' habitat, with large cavities and forks providing the best
roosting potential. Bats have voracious appetites and need to
consume a large volume of insects once they start hunting,

making woodland glades (which some gardens simulate very nicely) and ponds ideal hunting grounds.

The conservation threat posed to bats is reflected in the power of the legislation protecting them. As a European protected species, the implications for intentionally disturbing a bat roost or harming a bat are extremely serious, with potential for criminal prosecution. Any building or tree work carried out where there's either knowledge or a strong assumption of a bat presence should be planned in conjunction with a licensed, specialist bat handler, who can advise an approach to safeguard the bats – and your conscience. If you discover a bat roost while lagging a loft or pruning a large tree, the best approach.is always to stop and ask for advice.

An underrated threat to bats is another well-known mammal common in many homes, often answering to the name of 'Kitty'. The emergence of bats around dusk unfortunately coincides with cats departing for an evening's hunting. A very simple way to ensure your pet isn't responsible for the death of a protected species is to close upstairs windows as evening descends, and perhaps even keep the cat flap closed until it's fully dark and bats have left their roosts.

Bats love old characterful trees, so pruning and conserving veteran specimens in your garden is the right approach, with felling always a last resort. If a tree does have to come down, discuss the idea of a 'monolith' with your tree surgeon: a safe, standing section of trunk that still offers potential as a habitat, not just for bats, but nuthatches, woodpeckers and a vast array of invertebrates.

The size, complexity and long-term nature of maternity bat roosts means they're invariably sited in attics and large trees. There aren't many off-the-peg solutions for someone creating a maternity roost in their garden. There are, however, plenty of options for the smaller day and hibernation roosts, and bat boxes for individuals and small groups are widely available. These low-key structures are closed on three sides, with access to a narrow bottom entrance provided by a 'ladder' calibrated to scrabbling bat claws. Fix them high on a mature tree facing south for summer roosting (to keep the inhabitant as warm as possible) or north for winter (to ensure a stable hibernation not affected by fluctuating temperature), and site near an obvious food sources, such as an open area of wild flowers or a pond.

SHREWS (*Sorex* spp.)

One of the UK's smallest mammals, sightings of shrews are often limited to a scurrying brown shape on the garden path. Easily distinguished from mice, shrews have strong, oversized claws, long tails, a slender body with brown fur and – most distinctively – a long tapering snout (see colour section). Their young grow rapidly and can resemble their parents after as little as two weeks.

A relentless metabolism gives the shrew an insatiable appetite that needs constant servicing. Although not truly nocturnal, shrews are most active at night, and devote this time to constant foraging and eating. Slugs, moths, beetles and worms are preferred prey, making a useful contribution to pest control. If your garden is a true wildlife haven and home to a broad spectrum of wildlife, you may not mind supporting their predators, too, with the occasional shrew becoming prey to a barn owl, kestrel or grass snake.

HOW TO ENCOURAGE THEM: With an unquenchable desire for calories, the main requirement for any shrew in your garden is food and plenty of it. A wide variety of plants and habitats will create the right conditions for the invertebrates that compose the shrew's diet.

Although fast moving, and surprisingly aggressive, shrews are particularly vulnerable to attack from the air and unfortunately they're up against some foes with particularly sharp eyesight, such as kestrels and buzzards. Long grass makes an excellent haven from predators and this is one of many reasons why meadows are such desirable additions to your garden.

Dense vegetation may be suitable for a nest, although these are often dug underground. The shrew's metabolism and its lean build prevents it from getting fat and shutting down for the winter, so it remains active all year round.

Cats will always pose a threat to small mammals, and fitting them with a bell or excluding them from your garden altogether will avoid shrews becoming unnecessary prey.

However, shrews are also targeted by many other hunters and are easily frightened to death – reportedly even by thunder. They only live for less than a year, partly because they have such high metabolisms to fuel. Luckily for the species, they can have up to 18 offspring if able to survive a full year.

GARDEN BIRDS

ROBIN (*Erithacus rubecula*)

The air is cold, the ground is hard and the sky is grey. You're alone, a sole gardener against the elements, trying to get the bed dug, the fruit trees pruned or the compost heap turned. All of a sudden, your solitude is broken by a robin landing just a short distance away, perhaps the ultimate gardeners' friend. They don't combat disease or eat up all the slugs, but robins are there when we're slogging away in the garden or allotment, seemingly just keen to keep us company. Their rich song resonates in our ears throughout the winter (they're one of the few songbirds to maintain year-round territory) and their bright red plumage never stops looking striking (see colour section).

Robins are naturally birds of open woodland, but have adopted gardens as one of their preferred habitats. Living and nesting with us all year round, we can offer lots of help to ensure their ongoing success.

HOW TO ENCOURAGE THEM: Robins have a quirky, improvisational approach to nesting, choosing anything from an upturned plant pot to old wellies, and we may not realise where that cheeping sound was coming from until the last minute. If you've identified a nest, try to isolate it from disturbance, to prevent an unnerved mother deserting her clutch. Ready-made robin nest boxes have a wide open front and need a location that isn't too exposed either to predators or the sun. Place at about 2m (6ft) high, facing west into some vegetation cover. The ideal addition is a climber like ivy, which you can train to shelter the edges of the box without covering it completely.

Although robins obviously just like spending time with gardeners, there may be an ulterior motive. The digging we've just done is likely to have exposed a worm or two, and this encourages extraordinarily bold behaviour as robins dance around our feet, pulling their favourite food from the soil. For this reason, encouraging worms (see page 72) will help robins with a winter food source, although you may choose to supplement their wild foraging with high-energy snacks such as mealworms (available from specialist bird-food suppliers) or grated cheese.

SONG THRUSH (*Turdus philomelos*)

A tuneful source of pest control, this is a large songbird with a brown back and a pale yellow chest, speckled with black (see page 56 and colour section). The song thrush is a confident bird that skips around gardens with a positive, upright gait. Most memorable for its lyrical song composed of repeated phrases, it's often found in larger gardens with some tree cover.

Any gardener plagued by snails grazing their prize brassicas will welcome the appearance of a song thrush. Their fondness for one of the more devastating pests makes them a terrific friend and they're capable of maintaining a snail population at manageable, non-damaging levels.

Song thrushes are famed for using stones or paving as anvils against which to smash the snail's shell, allowing access to the juicy, protein-rich body within. This hard work is occasionally undermined: their cousin the blackbird has a reputation for nipping in and pinching the succulent snail once the thrush has done the hard work.

By nature, song thrushes are birds of open woodland and glades, which many gardens happily resemble. They prefer nesting in areas of dense undergrowth with a tree canopy above.

HOW TO ENCOURAGE THEM: Song thrushes need a reliable food source and a decent spot to nest if they're to establish themselves in your garden. As well as snails, song thrushes also like feeding on berries, so ensure any fruit you want to eat is netted – and consider leaving 'sacrificial' fruit bushes as a food source. Aside from raspberries and strawberries, there is a wide selection of garden trees and shrubs that song thrushes are very partial to, and will supplement their diet perfectly in the autumn. Oregon grape (*Mahonia aquifolium*) is tough, evergreen and perfect for a shady corner at the back of the garden. *Sorbus* is a dazzling genus of slender, garden-worthy trees, of which the native rowan is a member. Other trees and shrubs with thrush-friendly berries include cotoneaster, berberis and yew (*Taxus baccata*).

Apples make the perfect autumn feast for thrushes looking to build themselves up for the winter. If you're in the fortunate position of having an orchard, leave some windfalls on the ground. If not, try threading cored apples on to a stout piece of multi-ply garden twine (use fruits with some red colouration as it seems to stand out to the bird's eye). It might not only be the more common 'garden' thrushes that will descend; rarer migrants such as redwings and fieldfares could well be tempted in a harsh winter.

Encouraging wilder areas at the edge of the garden, preferably under trees, provides the ideal nesting spot with dense undergrowth and plenty of security from predators. If you can tolerate it, letting the brambles grow in your wilder corners allows for camouflaged foraging through your 'forest floor'.

If you feel that the thrushes aren't managing to deal with your snail problem sufficiently on their own, you can use an organic-approved slug and snail pellet (ferrous phosphate) in strict moderation to ensure that there's still some food available and that it's not toxic to the birds.

DOMESTIC BIRDS

CHICKENS (various breeds)

These provide great pest control and food recycling – and you'll save a fortune in eggs! Descended from jungle fowl, chickens were domesticated hundreds of years ago and have since metamorphosed into a bewildering array of shapes, sizes and colours, from the magnificent, exuberant Dorking (see page 59 and colour section) to the functional Black Rock.

The wonderfully omnivorous nature of a chicken will see it gobbling potato peelings and snails with almost equal relish. Feeding kitchen scraps to your chickens rather than putting them in landfill is kinder to the environment. And if you're happy to tolerate them wandering through your garden, chickens can act as a mobile pest patrol. But a chicken's ability to reduce any ground to bare soil through constant foraging and digging should be noted – the best way to incorporate these loveable birds into your garden is through regular rotation of their run, well away from any precious ornamental areas and seed beds.

Chicken welfare has become a hot political issue in recent times, with supermarkets under pressure to stop selling battery-reared eggs and birds. The simple fact is that chickens were once wild birds and placing them in an environment as restrictive as a battery crate is deeply unnatural. While commercially it may be a struggle to feed the UK solely with non-battery chickens, for the domestic bird-rearer, going free-range is a straightforward decision. Chickens are happy with a sturdy rain- and fox-proof house and a decent run so that they can stretch their legs, forage, dig for worms and take dust baths. If you want your birds to be truly free-range, there's something enduringly attractive about the sight of chickens on walls, roofs and cars. However, be aware that going down this route limits the protection you can offer them from predators and, of course, the eggs may be difficult to track down.

GETTING STARTED: There's a great selection of chicken accommodation available, from the achingly trendy Eglu to more traditional wooden houses to suit all garden sizes and budgets. As an approximate rule, allow a minimum of 1m (10¾ft) square per chicken when creating a run and remember the sheer willpower and ingenuity of their greatest foe, the fox, who is perfectly capable of digging under poorly fitted chicken wire or jumping inadequate fences. Ensure the top of the run is well covered and either dig the fence in or use a run with a stiff, dig-proof base.

Chickens are often sold as trios – two hens and one cock – and there's a certain domestic harmony that arises from this arrangement. Larger groups can become complex and the pecking order becomes very obvious. A cockerel isn't strictly necessary for egg production unless you intend to bring on more birds, but he will keep his hens in order and it is delightful to watch him breaking up the best of the kitchen scraps and offering the pieces to his ladies with encouraging clucking sounds.

Chickens will readily eat a wide variety of scraps, although they must never be fed any animal by-products by law. To ensure good health and consistent laying, supplement scraps with a poultry grain, mash or grit (containing crushed shells to cleanse the digestive tract). Chickens can get very thirsty in hot weather and need fresh water every day.

Rotating the location of their run doesn't just take the pressure off your garden, it also stops the parasites and diseases associated with poultry from building to dangerous levels in one location, and this is a fundamental part of hen husbandry.

INSECTS AND OTHER INVERTEBRATES

*A quiet revolution happened in gardening when
it was realised that invertebrates could be used to
control pests as effectively as chemicals. The result is
that many of the most intensively grown commercial crops,
such as glasshouse tomatoes, are produced with the
minimum of insecticides and with major assistance from
so-called 'biological controls' – and the great thing is
that domestic gardeners can get in on the act.*

With a combination of friendly invertebrates and the occasional squirt of gentle 'organic' insecticide, such as soap, you can keep your garden free of pest infestations and may never need to reach for the bug killer again. Beneficial insects such as lacewings and hoverflies are relatively easy to attract (or even buy) and we know enough about their likes and dislikes to ensure we can keep them hanging around.

The closer our garden can replicate a natural ecosystem, the healthier it will be. All elements of a food web are desirable, from predators that regulate our pest levels to recyclers such as stag beetles and earthworms.

PEST CONTROL

LACEWING (*Chrysopa* spp.)

Lacewings are long, slender and elegant, and the features
that give them their name seem almost implausibly delicate
(see colour section). While the adult lacewing feeds on nectar,
pollen and aphid 'honeydew' (a sugar-rich liquid excreted as
a waste product), its voracious, aggressive larvae consume
considerable volumes of garden pests. This curious split
in diet between larvae and adult is a clever evolutionary
adaptation common to many insects, to ensure one life
stage does not compete with the other for limited resources.

One of the most effective generalist predators in the garden,
lacewing larvae are also one of the few effective 'biological
controls' that you can buy to establish outdoors, in contrast
to the vast array of creatures available for glasshouses.

With the correct food source available at hatching, plus
reasonable shelter, lacewings should become resident in your
garden. Lacewing larvae can eat their way through hundreds
of aphids a week, and while this is their prime food source,
they also eat the equally pesky whitefly. The mode of action
for consuming aphids is grisly but effective: the larva injects
venom to paralyse its prey, then sucks out its bodily fluids,
leaving a dry husk.

HOW TO ENCOURAGE THEM: For adults to breed and become fully established in your garden, you'll need to provide shelter from harsh weather and winters. A lacewing habitat can be created using piles of dry twigs near pest-prone crops, or by purchasing a lacewing house (generally a stack of wooden or bamboo tubes).

Good organic-gardening catalogues and websites sell live lacewing larvae for garden introductions. Generally delivered in small plastic tubes, the larvae need to be gently tapped on to aphid-infested plants on a mild, still day between May and September.

Given their relative hardiness, lacewings should colonise fairly readily, although a second introduction may be required if there's no sign that they've overwintered.

HOVERFLY (*Syrphidae* family)

Although sometimes confused with wasps (a deliberate defensive strategy), their distinctive hovering flight and deep 'wing' buzz makes identification straightforward. Hoverflies also have big, spherical eyes, rounded stingless abdomens and mouthparts clearly designed to suck nectar, rather than rip flesh like a wasp.

Hoverflies are useful pollinators, but as with lacewings, it's their larvae that make them a most potent garden friend. A hoverfly larva (or maggot) can eat 300–500 aphids during this life stage, before pupating and turning into an adult, when it goes on to pollinate the plants it has been protecting.

Where hoverflies really excel is in the management of mass aphid outbreaks: the mobility of the adult, early hatching and the prolific appetite of the larvae combine to create a rapid-reaction force. This response can visibly reduce an aphid population in a few days and stop serious, long-term damage to your plants.

HOW TO ENCOURAGE THEM: Hoverflies are a typical sight in summer and tend to be most active above 15°C (59°F). High humidity encourages hoverflies to emerge from the pupae. The diversity of heights and flowers in a domestic garden offers a good habitat, although the larvae aren't keen to crawl along the stems of hairy-leaved plants.

Hoverflies, particularly the species *Episyrphus balteatus* (see colour section), can be bought as a biological control, mail-order from good organic-gardening catalogues and websites. The larvae need shelter, warmth and humidity to establish and plenty of nectar-rich plants should be available for the adults to feed on.

LADYBIRD (*Coccinellidae* family)

Ladybirds complete this potent trio of native pest controllers. If you're lucky enough to have ladybirds, lacewings and hoverflies in your garden, aphids and their kind will never take the upper hand. There are 42 species of ladybird in the UK, distinguished by spot pattern and numbers, and the colour of their elytra, or wing cases (see colour section). The alien harlequin ladybird (large, with 15–21 spots) has been the focus of attention recently.

The vivid colourings advertise a bitter, unpleasant experience for any predator daring to attack and ladybirds have relatively few enemies – although they sometimes clash with ants, which 'farm' aphids in return for rich drops of honeydew. While ladybirds are a colourful, cheery presence in any garden, it's their larvae that help gardeners most. Looking like a different species entirely, their powerful jaws and dark, spiky, segmented bodies give them a menacing appearance.

Just like lacewings and hoverflies, ladybirds and their larvae consume significant volumes of aphids and whitefly – enough to get a serious pest outbreak under control. Additional benefits include the willingness and mobility of the adult ladybirds as pollinators, plus they maintain their appetite for aphids once metamorphosed.

HOW TO ENCOURAGE THEM: While you may want voracious ladybird larvae to get stuck into your aphid infestation immediately, they won't arrive of their own volition. Your first task is to make your garden attractive to the adults. Provide lots of their favourite nectar-rich plants: outstanding choices include yarrow (*Achillea millefolium*), tansy (*Tanacetum vulgare*) and cosmos. Adult ladybirds will also need convincing that your garden is a good place to survive a harsh winter, so provide shelter in the form of dead hedges, wood stacks, dead flower stems or even a purpose-built ladybird house. It's easy enough to buy or make: a log with deep holes drilled into it – around 5mm (¼in) in diameter – or a bundle of dry, fully hollow bamboo canes hung somewhere dry and sheltered will provide a suitable haven for overwintering ladybirds to wiggle safely and snugly into.

POLLINATORS

WASP (*Vespula vulgaris*)

Common wasps are powerful predators, readily distinguished by their powerful jaws, strong flight, sharply tapering abdomens and familiar colour scheme of yellow and black (see following page and colour section). They are sociable insects living together in colonies.

What good is a wasp? A question posed by many, perhaps after being stung or having a late summer picnic blighted by the unwanted attentions of these apparently malevolent insects. In fact, there is much to be gained from having wasps in your garden: they're surprisingly effective pollinators, recyclers and pest controllers.

Wasps keep a low profile in the first half of the summer; the main role of the male workers is to find protein in the form of carrion or live prey to feed to the growing grubs back in the nest. At this stage, they're undoubtedly garden friends, feeding extensively on aphids and whitefly and cheerily tidying death and decay from the garden.

By late summer, their work is done. The grubs have hatched and the colonies break up, leaving hordes of disaffected males kicking their heels and searching for the sugary high once provided by the grubs in return for being fed. Only at this stage do they lapse from friend to irritation, dive-bombing picnics, landing in our food and stinging us as we flap our hands to wave them away...

Wasps are cosmopolitan and have adapted to a wide range of habitats, both wild and man-made. They need a source of wood pulp for their nests, somewhere warm for the queen to hibernate and a good source of protein for their grubs.

HOW TO TOLERATE THEM: While anyone starting a business selling mail-order wasps or nests may struggle financially, the main point is, surely, how to tolerate the wasps already established in your garden, given the benefits they bestow. Some people seem compelled to wave their arms around as wasps start to circle, but this only serves to antagonise. Irritated wasps emit pheromones to communicate their stress to other wasps and this can lead to a more concerted attack.

If you live for alfresco dining but want to do so in peace, try to persuade wasps away from your table. Lures fashioned from plastic bottles and filled with sugar syrup in a location away from where you're eating may distract wasps enough to make dining comfortable. If it's sugar they're after, why not eat your savoury courses outside and retire indoors for dessert?

BEE (*Apis, Bombus* and *Osmia* spp.)

Several species of bee are regularly spotted in gardens. Mason bees (*Osmia* spp.) are easily distinguished from honeybees by their red-orange colouring and solitary disposition. Bumblebees (*Bombus* spp.) nest communally but forage alone, venturing out as soon as winter starts turning to spring and renowned for their 'bumbling' flight pattern. Honeybees (*Apis* spp.) are generally placid unless defending a hive and this is where an evolutionary flaw is revealed. Their sting was designed for killing other bees during 'turf wars' between hives, and when attacking a thick, flexible-skinned mammal, the abdominal foundation of the stinger can be ripped out, killing the bee.

Bees are inextricably linked to human survival. Their prowess as pollinators, and the plants they choose to pollinate, deliver staple foods for populations all over the planet from okra to kiwi, cashew to tomato, apple to guava and thousands more. Replicating the effect of bee pollination is extremely difficult on a modest domestic scale and physically impossible on a large commercial one.

Bees have made the headlines recently for all the wrong reasons. Their global health is in acute decline, and worryingly, we're not entirely sure why. In the case of honeybees, it's true that the rise of the parasitic *Varroa* mite and the disease they bring, varroatosis, is clearly identified as weakening and killing individual bees, but it's the sinister, inexplicable sudden Colony Collapse Disorder that threatens global agriculture.

Scientists, fuelled by intense public interest, government support and a very real threat to the global agricultural economy, are trying to analyse everything that might cause beekeepers to find their hives full of dead bees in the spring.

HOW TO ENCOURAGE THEM: Mason bees live in hollow plant stems such as reeds, or holes in trees or standing wood, which they often line with mud, hence their name. Mason bee nests are easy to build and even easier to buy. Bamboo canes, dried reeds or drilled timber rounds make viable homes, although the size of the entry hole is critical, with 2–10mm ($\frac{1}{16}$–$\frac{3}{8}$in) being ideal. A south-facing aspect is vital for siting the bee house, preferably with some protection from the rain. Mason bees need the warmth of the sun to thrive and will struggle to overwinter in a cold, damp spot.

Bumblebees nest sociably, underground and are often at the mercy of raids from protein-hungry badgers. Ready-made nests can be bought, as can the bees themselves – they're often used as the pollinator of choice in commercial tomato production. A home-made bumblebee house could be a shallow hole in the ground, lined with chicken wire or gauze and then padded with some dry straw. An upside-down terracotta pot over the top completes the shelter, while a short length of pipe, partly buried, leading out of the nest and emerging from the soil nearby will allow for protected access in and out.

Other species of bee, such as the tawny mining bee (*Andrena fulva*) also nest in soil and their presence is indicated by cone-shaped mounds of earth in lawns and sandy soils. This useful pollinator is a clear garden friend, and prefers steep banks and minimal vegetation.

Honeybees are gregarious insects, living in large, sophisticated colonies that are, of course, often created and managed by us. In the wild they chose venues such as hollow trees for their nests. Keeping honeybees is a significant but extremely pleasurable undertaking. Wherever you live in the country or city, there will be a beekeeping club or association nearby and they're often looking for enthusiastic new members. Your local beekeeping association will also be able to advise on courses run by the British Beekeeping Association to help budding beekeepers develop the basic competencies to manage hives, as well as more advanced skills for the future.

RECYCLERS

STAG BEETLES (*Lucanus cervus*)

Known in legend as summoners of thunder and lightning, stag beetles may appear intimidating with their extraordinary jaws – although these are used solely to determine strength and virility between jousting males (see colour section). Measuring up to 9cm (3½in) in length, this is Britain's largest beetle, and its complex habitat requirements and long lifecycle have put it under pressure to survive.

The stag beetle's lifecycle involves breaking down rotting wood and other plant detritus into its constituent elements: humic matter and a rich array of nutrients, released from forms unavailable to plants into an easy-to-assimilate one. This essential service stimulates new life and increased plant health and makes for good housekeeping.

Eggs are laid deep in dead wood, where the larvae hatch and feed, digesting cellulose and lignin before eventually migrating to the soil where they pupate into adults.

Some insects, notably the aphid, have extraordinarily short lifecycles, turning whole generations around in five days (when conditions are perfect, female aphids are born pregnant). Not the stag beetle, whose larvae can take up to six years to mature. Herein lies the threat to their survival. Finding the quality and continuity of habitat for this extraordinary lifecycle to develop is unusual, although well-informed park keepers, gardeners and wildlife-reserve managers strive to support stag beetles. However, the overall picture for stag beetles is a challenging one, with pressure on their habitat from development, changing land use and a natural human instinct to clear away dead wood threatening its survival.

HOW TO ENCOURAGE THEM: Although they are uncommon, well-managed gardens can be a haven for stag beetles and may be their best option to survive and establish a viable population, particularly in the south east. The national stag beetle survey conducted in 2002 recorded 75 per cent of beetle sightings in gardens and this gives gardeners a real opportunity to help sustain a threatened species. To create the potential for stag beetles comes down to how you manage dead wood: the type of wood you leave, where it is left and the way it is stacked.

The best wood comes from broadleaf trees, which sustain a greater diversity of species than coniferous wood, with oak and fruit trees being particularly good. Leave the bark on and site the wood out of full sun. This enables it to retain its natural moisture (to support wood-chewing beetles and their larvae) and a shady spot avoids it becoming fully seasoned. Form the wood into stacks. Vertical stacks of stout logs or cordwood, at least 10cm (4in) in diameter should contain varying heights of 30–100cm (1–3ft). Burying up to a third of the logs underground will draw damp up from the soil to keep the logs moist, and attract soil-dwelling beetles and fungi. Choose a site where the stack won't be disturbed or suddenly become exposed to full sun and wait.

Adult stag beetles essay a lazy flight in mid- to late summer looking for a suitable mate, and females lay eggs by the end of the season.

WORMS

Earthworm (*Lumbricus* spp.)

Earthworms are limbless, segmented invertebrates that live predominantly underground. Abundant in most gardens, they make a vital contribution to the ecology and balance of the soil and are like mobile recycling units.

Earthworms can process vast volumes of soil and organic matter to improve the structure of your garden, turning organic matter (such a dry leaves sitting on the surface of a lawn) into humus, a rich substance vital for good plant life. At the same time their insatiable taste for dirt and a grit-lined gut allows them to process large lumps of soil into fine 'crumbs', improving the structure of the earth and allowing plant roots to move more freely and access soil and nutrients more readily. It's no exaggeration to state that earthworms are essential to healthy soil.

Yet worm casts are a source of great angst to some. The appearance of casts on golf courses and football pitches, where cylinder mowers turn them into unsightly smears, earns the earthworm the unlikely status of pest, and worm killers are deployed to eliminate them. To the domestic gardener however, worm casts are a blessing, being richly concentrated sources of humus and nutrients. If collected in sufficient volume, worm casts can be used as an additive to potting compost or as the basis for 'worm tea'.

This surreal-sounding brew is simply worm casts steeped in water, an effective way to distribute their rich properties around your garden. It needn't be an exact science: a few handfuls of casts wrapped in permeable fabric and immersed in at least 10 litres (2 gallons) of water for 24 hours will create a useful concentrate. Keeping the solution warm in a shed or garage and bubbling oxygen through using an aquarium pump will make it significantly more potent. Dilute at a ratio of one part tea to ten parts water and apply to lawns, shrubs, roses, fruit, vegetables and bedding plants.

HOW TO ENCOURAGE THEM: Worms tolerate a wide range of soils but are happiest in free-draining ground. Given their ability to improve soil structure, they're most desirable to the gardener on heavier clays or loams. To ensure a healthy, effective population of earthworms under your feet, it's important to understand what might deter or kill them.

They can drown in heavily waterlogged ground; adding organic matter, gravel or regular spiking of the lawn will reduce this threat. Worms are also extremely sensitive to changes in the salt, pH or chemical balance of the soil. Frequent or excessive use of inorganic (chemical-based) fertilisers, pesticides or herbicides can significantly affect soil chemistry and create a hostile environment for worms and other desirable invertebrates and microbes.

AMPHIBIANS AND REPTILES

We've looked at how friendly insects help deal with problems like aphids and whitefly. Now it's the turn of larger-scale pest control in the form of big-hitting amphibians and reptiles, such as toads and slow worms. Their ability to consume large quantities of slugs endears them to any gardener and it's worth boosting their habitat requirements – your garden may be more suitable than you think.

TOAD (*Bufo bufo*)

'If only something would come and eat slugs' is a thought many of us have had after surveying devastated hostas or cabbages. Enter one of the ultimate garden friends: the toad. Their habitat requirements are a little specialised, and it may take some time to encourage them into your garden, but if you're lucky enough to have a resident toad, you'll have a most potent source of pest control. Their appetite is voracious and also extends to flying ants, flies, centipedes and the dreaded mosquitoes.

Easily distinguished from frogs, toads have dry, warty skin, thickset bodies and a slow, deliberate walk (see opposite and colour section). Their eggs or spawn are laid in long strings (as opposed to the clumps produced by frogs) and their tadpoles are plain dark brown – frog tadpoles are freckled. Toadlets emerge in late July.

Although toads need water to reproduce – travelling 1km (½ mile) or more to return to the same pond each year – they spend much time on land and their warty skin allows them to tolerate relatively dry conditions.

HOW TO ENCOURAGE THEM: Toads are nocturnal, just like slugs, and one of their chief requirements is a cool, shady place to shelter during the heat of the day. Toad shelters don't need to be high-tech. Utilise porous, toad-friendly terracotta by pushing half of a broken clay plant pot into the soil in a shady spot, leaving a narrow, semicircular entrance. Line the shelter's floor with some leaf litter and moss for toad comfort. While it's not essential for your garden to have a pond to host toads, there will need to be one within waddling distance for them to breed and become truly established. So if you have the room, and fancy a challenge, why not create a small, wildlife-focused pond? It won't just benefit toads – you could end up attracting frogs, newts, pond skaters, dragonflies and swallows into the bargain.

It's important to select a good site for your pond, preferably south facing, so the water warms up quickly in the spring by absorbing any heat from a weak winter sun. A situation protected from chilly easterly and northerly winds will enhance this effect. Ponds need a minimum depth of at least 50cm (20in) to be effective for wildlife and to resist rapid evaporation. Whether to line it or not will depend on your soil. Heavy clay can be smeared or 'puddled' to create an effective seal, although this could crack open during prolonged periods of drought. Lighter, sandier soils with no binding capacity may need a synthetic liner – butyl or the more sophisticated EPDM are good choices.

Ponds need to be physically diverse, with a variety of depths to support a broad range of wildlife. Boggy, marginal areas allow plants such as flag iris (*Iris pseudacorus*) and kingcup (*Caltha palustris*) to establish, while shallow areas of warm water make good locations for frog and toad spawn. Stacks of wood or dry-stone walls at the pond edge make great transitional habitats for invertebrates and amphibians, while submerged vegetation, such as water-lilies (*Nymphaea* spp.) will not only balance the ecology of the pond, but also provide a location for aquatic insects to lay eggs.

Slow worm (*Anguis fragilis*)

One of the more obscure elements of our native fauna,
slow worms are surprisingly common in gardens. They are
slender, legless lizards that can reach 45cm (18in) in length.
Commonly mistaken for snakes, they are distinguished by
the presence of eyelids and the ability to shed their tail as
an escape mechanism, although this should never be put
to the test – slow worms are a protected species.

Gardens in which slugs and snails are dominant aren't just
unfortunate, they're ecologically unbalanced, with an absence
of effective mollusc predators to stop numbers getting out of
hand. A viable population of slow worms will graze slug and
snail numbers and maintain them below the levels that can
devastate hostas and broccoli overnight.

HOW TO ENCOURAGE THEM: Slow worms are low-key,
secretive reptiles and you may have them in your garden
without realising it. Their inability to generate body heat
means they prefer warmer sandy soil and need a good
south- or west-facing basking spot, although they'll never
choose a site too exposed to predators. Their secretive
dispositions and the vulnerability of their young means they
need good shelter, such as long meadow grass, hedgerows or
open shrub beds (replicating heathland). Anywhere too cool
or dark isn't suitable, although they do like to laze under slate,
corrugated iron or even in a black plastic plant tray as these
items will heat up in the sun and provide a cosy retreat.

NATURAL INFLUENCES

*You've welcomed friendly wildlife into your garden
with open arms and cultivated plants that will do
everything from deterring pests to attracting pollinating
insects. But there are still a few more aspects of nature
that you can harness to help you in the garden; from
composting and hanging on to dead wood to
studying the phases of the moon.*

DEAD WOOD

Although a garden full of healthy, living plants is always
desirable, there's plenty of merit in encouraging a bit of
death too. In wild ecosystems, live and dead organic matter
coexist, and it's generally our natural desire to tidy up our
gardens that upsets this balance.

Dead wood is an immensely rich habitat, capable of
supporting an extraordinary suite of different animals,
fungi and microorganisms. In finding clever ways to keep
some in your garden, you can do wonders for biodiversity
without compromising on appearances. Many species of beetle
base their lifecycles around dead wood, laying their eggs in
fallen trunks and branches, and the emerging larvae feed on
decaying woody matter. Many fungi need dead wood in their
lifecycle and providing some in your garden can attract
desirable mycorrhizal fungi that may benefit your plants.
Dead wood stacks and 'dead hedges' (see opposite) provide
safe, shady, temperature-regulated sanctuaries from the outside
world and the threat of predators. For this reason, they're

often chosen as the ideal winter residence by amphibians such as newts, mammals such as dormice, voles and beneficial insects such as mason bees, lacewings and ladybirds.

DEAD HEDGES AND WOOD STACKS

Being comfortable with the sight of stacks of dead wood may mean adjusting your tolerance levels, and employing creative ideas that don't affect the overall aesthetic of your garden. It's in our nature to be tidy, and dead wood may instinctively feel like mess that needs to be cleared. However, with such rich wildlife benefits, it's worth trying out dead hedges and wood stacks to see what they'll attract to your garden.

Dead hedges don't sound terribly inspiring, but they can make a really dynamic statement if done well. Composed of dense horizontal layers of dead branches, brash and leaves, they are secured by stout, rustic upright poles, preferably cut from the same material (see colour section). They can be curved into sinuous, flowing lines: you could use them to denote the transition in your garden between 'high horticulture' and a more relaxed, wildlife-friendly area.

The very nature of the material will make the dead hedge brittle over time and it will need occasional rebuilding and resetting. This is best done in the middle of spring, when your overwintering guests have emerged and before anything contemplates nesting in it.

If you simply want to leave some dead wood stacked around the place, this will offer the same ecological benefits. Banging in some upright posts either side of the stack will stop it from collapsing, if you have young, adventurous children. More information about wood stacks is given on page 71.

COMPOST

There are few substances more friendly to your garden than compost. Either as a mulch, soil improver, source of beneficial bacteria and fungi or simply the most economic, efficient way to deal with garden waste, this is a versatile, desirable product that's easy to make (see page 82).

MULCHING

Mulching boosts the health of plants, improves your soil and suppresses weeds. On hot days, the heat of the sun on the ground forces moisture to evaporate from roots near the surface, placing undue stress on the plant. A thick layer of good compost around the plant creates an insulating barrier, isolating the roots from extreme variations in temperature and making drought less stressful. The secondary benefit of mulch is that it acts as a smothering layer, stopping any annual weed seed in the soil from germinating, although this technique will not work against perennial weeds like dandelions, which will simply force their way through.

IMPROVING THE SOIL

Most soils can be improved with the addition of compost.
Add thick layers while digging, cultivating ground or planting.
Organic matter can open up soil structures to allow more
consistent drainage, create greater bulk in thin soils to increase
water retention, or disrupt the thick, 'clodding' nature of
heavy clay.

Good compost is teeming with desirable biology. Every garden
has its own unique flora: not just the visible garden plants
we've carefully chosen, but a second microscopic one: bacteria
(including *Bacillus subtilis*, see page 41), fungi and protozoa
(single-celled microscopic organisms). When our 'microflora'
is functioning well, it becomes an active garden friend,
competing with diseases to stop them taking over, helping
plants make better use of water and making nutrients more
available by converting them to useful plant-friendly forms.
With a good 'microflora' in place, it's highly desirable to find
ways to perpetuate it. By recycling garden waste, rather than
throwing it away, we can keep these invisible but highly
desirable elements in our garden. Tests on best-quality
home-made garden compost have revealed desirable
microbes in wonderful abundance.

MAKING COMPOST

For garden waste to become compost, some simple rules
need to be adhered to. A good ratio of green (weeds, grass,
herbaceous material) to brown (prunings, straw, dry leaves,
cardboard) waste will activate composting bacteria and fungi.
While two parts brown to one part green is the ultimate ratio,
simply ensuring a balance of the two elements will improve
your compost greatly.

Getting the moisture levels right is vital: too dry and there'll
be no composting reaction; too wet and it will be the wrong
sort, leading to damp, smelly stuff with little use. Ideally your
compost should be about 50 per cent moist, and this is best
revealed by the simple 'squeeze test'. Squeeze a handful of
compost and it should bind together a little, not crumble
away. Your hand should feel moist, but on no account should
water be dripping down your arm. The best way to ensure
good moisture levels is regular watering in dry weather and
a tarpaulin to stop waterlogging during downpours.

THE TURNOVER

There's not always the space to do it, but any efforts to turn
or mix your compost will improve it greatly. It might be the
physical action of your fork, breaking down stubborn lumps,
the airing your compost receives as you open it up, or the
mixing process, but turning is a guaranteed way to speed up
production. Building a couple of open bays, side by side, to
hold your compost heaps, makes turning much easier. Lifting
and throwing forkfuls of compost from full bay to empty,
allows the creation of a new heap. A regular garden fork will

do the job, but a genuine pitchfork (with curved tines and pointy ends) will make life even easier. Where there isn't the space for this type of system, or if the gardener lacks the strength or inclination for all that turning, a tumbler-style composter offers the ideal alternative and has the added benefit of being rodent-proof.

MAKING LEAF MOULD

If you have a significant volume of leaves landing on your garden in autumn, it's worth creating a dedicated leaf-mould pile. This marvellous stuff tends to be denser, richer and with a lower pH than green-waste compost, especially if beech leaves or pine needles are the main constituent. Leaf mould lends itself to specialist applications such as planting, propagation and mulching of ericaceous (acid-loving) shrubs like rhododendrons. To make good leaf mould, rake your leaves into rows and run a rotary mower over them before stacking in an open heap. The blades of the mower chop thick, difficult-to-rot leaves into fine shreds while collecting a small volume of grass. The grass adds nitrogen to the carbon-rich leaf mix and a desirable composting environment is created, speeding up the process of decay – turning one autumn's leaves into the following spring's leaf mould. Leaving your leaf heap exposed to the elements seems to suit the process, so don't worry about it getting wet.

Composting kitchen waste

Food is traditionally thought of as being hard to compost, but invest a little money, and this waste stream suddenly becomes a useful addition to your garden. Rather than using open bays for food composting, buy a fit-for-purpose 'closed' composter designed to either rot food waste down to nothing, or employing insulation and engineering to ensure the end product is thoroughly processed and safe. Green Cones and Green Johannas are usually available for a small investment from local authorities keen to reduce their landfill contribution. They both take the full range of food waste, including meat, fish and dairy. Green Johannas require the addition of garden compost, need to be in the shade and create a composted end product; Green Cones turn the waste to a negligible residue.

A more sophisticated solution, Swedish tumbler composters such as the Jora can turn a wide variety of food waste into really good compost. Thick foam insulation, a tight seal and 'blanking plates' that allow one side of the tumbler to be emptied at a time, ensure a really good composting temperature and ease of use. Spending a few hundred pounds on one of these could transform what you put in your landfill bin and give you some excellent compost for the garden. When processed well, food-waste compost is fine, dark and crumbly with a surprisingly high level of nutrients. The purchase of a decent probe thermometer is recommended to ensure you're getting composting temperatures of 60°C (140°F) or more, reassuring you that bacteria have been killed.

PLANTING BY THE MOON

Have you read that right? Surely abstract astrology has nothing to do with a practical book about gardening? Well, strangely enough, there's more than just hippy wisdom behind paying heed to the moon and its potential influence over your garden and its plantlife.

Many civilisations, including the ancient Egyptians and native Americans, have worked around lunar cycles, using different phases to plant specific crops, and there's a growing interest in the principle now. Although chiefly adopted by the biodynamic movement, a highly developed form of gardening and farming with a strong spiritual and metaphysical element, there's no reason why the occasional use of a lunar planting calendar can't be employed to improve potential crop health and productivity. Crop research stations have decades of data on the influence of the moon over our crops and it might be worth investigating the work of Maria Thun and others to make your own mind up.

To follow lunar planting and sowing cycles, you need to buy one of the many annual guides that converts astrological information into practical guidance, offering not only the best time to plant, but also to weed, water and fertilise. The essence of lunar planting is this: over any month, the gravitational effect of the moon on water-table and sap levels varies to the point that different types of crop have favourable days to be planted, harvested and even eaten.

Leaf crops such as lettuce keep most of their watery mass above the soil and need moisture to establish quickly. If the water table is high, by this logic, the leaf crop should have good access to it and be extra succulent.

When the water table is low, this suits root crops, such as parsnips, which need most of their moisture deep in the soil.

Two additional monthly phases, flower and fruit days, sit within these two extremes of water table and, providing these windows of planting opportunity don't occur at 2am on a Sunday morning, what could be more interesting than some domestic experimentation to support or debunk the notion of moon planting?

Plant a control crop that takes no heed of interplanetary alignment and compare with your moon-planted crop. Which one has more flowers and fruit? Which plant develops a bigger root mass? How tall and wide do they grow?

AND FINALLY...

*If you feel inspired to attract some new friends
into your garden, there can be no simpler principle
than understanding your garden habitat and
cross-referencing with the needs of your
would-be residents.*

Some alterations may be simple and effective, others may
require lots of work and take many years to be successful
but ultimately, even the smallest concession to nature will
be richly rewarding.

FURTHER READING

Adams, C.R., Early, M.P., and Bamford, K.M., *Principles of Horticulture*, 5th Edition (Butterworth-Heinemann, 2008)

Carroll, Steven B. and Salt, Steven D., *Ecology for Gardeners* (Timber Press, 2004)

Davies, Andrew, *Beekeeping: Inspiration and Practical Advice for Would-be Smallholders* (National Trust Books, 2007)

Eastoe, Jane, *Allotments* (National Trust Books, 2009)

Galligan, Diana *Home Grown Vegetables: Inspiration and Practical Advice for Would-be Smallholders* (National Trust Books, 2007)

Ikin, Ed, *Thoughtful Gardening* (National Trust Books, 2010)

Jonsson, Lars, *Birds of Europe: with North Africa and the Middle East* (Helm, 2005)

King, John, *Reaching for the Sun: How Plants Work*, 2nd edition (Cambridge University Press, 2011)

Lavell, Mick, *101 Ideas for a Wildlife Friendly Garden* (Gardeners' World Magazine, BBC Books 2009)

Lowenfels, Jeff and Lewis, Wayne, *Teaming with Microbes: A Gardener's Guide to the Soil Food Web* (Timber Press, 2006)

Mabey, Richard, *Weeds: How vagabond plants gatecrashed civilisation and changed the way we think about nature* (Profile Books, 2010)

McLaren, Chris, *Ponds: Creating and Maintaining a Wildlife Pond* (National Trust Books, 2009)

Newland, David, *Britain's Butterflies* (Wild Guides, 2010)

Thomas, Adrian, *RSPB Gardening for Wildlife: A Complete Guide to Nature-friendly Gardening* (A&C Black, 2010)

Thompson, Ken, *No Nettles Required: The Reassuring Truth About Wildlife Gardening* (Eden Project Books 2007)

Wilson, Bee, *The Hive: The Story of the Honeybee and Us* (John Murray, 2004)

GOOD SUPPLIERS AND
USEFUL WEBSITES

ASTON HORTICULTURE
(www.astonhorticulture.com)
A company trying to wean UK horticulture off pesticides
and on to garlic. This website provides lots of additional
information about the role of garlic in controlling pests
and disease and details the products Aston manufactures.

BUGLIFE
(www.buglife.org.uk)
A vibrant charity supporting conservation work not just
for bugs but all invertebrates. The website is packed with
information and practical advice on supporting invertebrates
in your garden, with opportunities to get involved in
Europe-wide surveys.

CHILTERNS SEEDS
(www.chilternseeds.co.uk)
A great horticultural institution, Chilterns sells a terrific array
of garden seeds, from heritage cottage-garden snapdragons
antirrhinums to the latest wild-collected exotica from Chile
and South Africa. All your pollinator-friendly plants are
available from this likeable family-run firm.

ECOLOGICAL PARTNERSHIPS
(www.nationaltrustwildlifehabitats.co.uk)
Wildlife Habitats works in partnership with the National Trust to produce a range of renewable, sustainable and ethically produced wild-animal habitats, bird boxes, feeders, tables and wild-bird food.

GARDEN ORGANIC
(www.gardenorganic.org.uk)
A committed, passionate charity organisation offering a positive green influence to British gardeners. The company's catalogue is full of useful alternatives to conventional pesticides and fertilisers and their list of biological controls (such as lacewings) is second to none.

GARDENING NATURALLY
(www.gardening-naturally.com)
Retailers and manufacturers who are supporting the movement away from fungicide-based gardening. There's a huge range of products available, and all provide effective ways to facilitate organic gardening, from *Bacillus subtilis* solutions to sterilising solutions for cleaning plant pots without bleach.

JUST GREEN
(www.just-green.com)
A wide range of practically focused green products, including natural pest control, plants and gardening equipment.

LANDLIFE

(www.wildflower.co.uk)

A highly innovative organisation dedicated to conserving our wild flowers and bringing them to a wider audience. Its work introducing wild flower meadows to desolate urban sites has shown the positive influence of plants on people's lives. Its range of wildflower seed is excellent, as is its landmark wildflower centre in Liverpool.

RSPB

(www.rspb.org.uk)

'Britain's voice for nature' is a large but highly effective organisation that campaigns avidly to conserve our birdlife and also works on broader nature-conservation issues. The RSPB range of bird food and feeders is exceptional.

SIMPSONS SEEDS

(www.simpsonsseeds.co.uk)

We're lucky to have the choice of so many fantastic seed suppliers in this country. From household names to specialist high-end firms specialising in regional Italian vegetables, there's a catalogue for everyone. However, if I had to order all my vegetables and herbs from just one supplier, I would make it Simpsons, which maintains just the right balance between traditional varieties, new trends and staple crops. Their service is second to none.

SMARTSOIL

(www.smartsoil.co.uk)

Distributor of food-waste tumbler composters in the UK. The company stocks two sizes of the domestic-scale tumbler and offers a mail-order service. For larger scale or commercial food-waste composting, try Magna Composting (www.magnacompost.co.uk) which provides composters, monitoring equipment, technical expertise and their own compost.

THE WILDLIFE TRUST

(www.wildlifetrust.org)

The Trust manages thousands of nature reserves, provides education and training and expert advice to any wildlife query. Its children's membership is particularly rewarding, with an excellent magazine.

WIGGLY WIGGLERS

(www.wigglywigglers.co.uk)

This company has expanded from selling wormeries to covering all green-living needs. Ethically sourced products, green pest control and lots of wildlife gardening accessories can be found in its comprehensive catalogue and website.

INDEX